Legendary
Performance

Pattiann Rogers (signature)

Pattiann Rogers

Gettysburg, PA (handwritten)
9/22/92 (handwritten)

Ion Books/ Raccoon
Memphis, Tennessee

Ion Books/*Raccoon*
3387 Poplar Avenue, Suite 205
Memphis, TN 38111

A Raccoon Book

Library of Congress Cataloging-in-Publication Data

Rogers, Pattiann, 1940-
    Legendary Performance

I. Title
    PS3568.0454L4   1987   811'.54   86-33755

ISBN 0-938507-07-9

Cover photograph by Eddy Cothey

Book design by David Spicer & Diana Taylor

Acknowledgements

My thanks to the editors of the following magazines in which many of these poems first appeared:

Amelia: "The Myth: Raison d'Être"
American Poetry Review: "Sight and Sound"
Chiaroscuro: "Albert, Standing in the Forest at Night, Asks Himself, 'Where Did I Come From?'"
Chicago Review: "After Dinner," "Aspects of Unity," and "A Seasonal Tradition"
Chowder Review: "Gentlemen of Leisure" and "The Truth of the Matter"
Columbia: "Naked Boys on Naked Ponies"
Domestic Crude: "A Modicum of Decorum"
The Hiram Poetry Review: "The Creation of Sin"
image: "The Clockmaker and the Toymaker Are Friends" and "The Effort to Eliminate Ignorance: Birdwatching"
Iowa Review: "Entomological Research" and "The Structure of Sustenance"
Kayak: "A Fortnight to Remember," "Seminar," "The Pursuit as Solution," and "The Shape of Sorrow"
Missouri Review: "How the Whale Forgets the Love of Felicia"
Nimrod: "The Documentation of Absence"
Poetry Miscellany: "Locating the Source of Intention," "The Facts of the Earth," and "One in Three"
Poetry Now: "The Mystery of Union"
Prairie Schooner: "The Witness of Death," "The Well-Wisher from Half-Way Around the World," "Being Remembered," and "The Evolution of Freedom"
Palmetto Review: "The Mirror of Pierrot"
Seattle Review: "The Love of Enchantment: Felicia Was Kissed in the Garden Last Night"
Southern Review: "The Revelation of the Willed Hallucination" and "The Study of the Splinter Expert"

"The Evolution of Freedom" also appeared in the chapbook, *The Only Holy Window,* Trilobite Press.

Special thanks to the John Simon Guggenheim Foundation and the National Endowment for the Arts for fellowships which provided support and encouragement during the period when many of these poems were written.

To Cynthia Macdonald and Elizabeth McBride, my loving thanks for careful reading and for encouragement and support of these poems.

For my sons, John A. and Arthur

Contents

Part I

After Dinner

Cecil said, "During every night and every day
Of the evolving invention and increased usage
Of the table fork, during every moment and every note
Of the Bach missa performed for the king of Saxony
Before his fire in 1733, through the long rising popularity
Of croquet, played by many fine ladies during summer evenings
In smooth grassy gardens, the light from the exploding
Supernova located in the exterior Galaxy M31 was steadily
Proceeding at 186,000 miles per second straight toward
1929 and Edwin Hubble and his telescope right here on earth."

Sonia said, "If you picture the progress of your thought
As a wooden ball rolling heavily over grass, clearing
Two wire wickets cleanly, then striking a stake with decision,
You might come to understand some totally unexpected truth."

"During every moment of every word of Cecil's speech,"
Albert said, "the weaver ants on the bush beside this bench
Were sewing together two separate leaves by the perfect
Needle and thread of their children's bodies."

"Look at Felicia, having won at croquet, cartwheeling
Across the hill, her feet sweeping in finite arcs
Through every second of the heavens from Capricornus
To Sextanus, from Altair to Corvus."

Gordon, who is writing an article
On stitching of any kind, adds four new elements
To his thesis every evening.

A Fortnight to Remember

Cecil's second cousin has a handicap.
An incurable condition, he can't distinguish
Between his memory and his imagination.

Arriving for a two-week visit, he thinks
He came by circling out of the center
Of the high bush blueberry blooming at the gate.
Later that evening he amused everyone by recounting
The adventures of a confused passenger
On an imaginary train trip.

Believing the winding staircase and the red carpeted
Hallway leading to the guest bedroom to be stanzas
In his newest poem, he has slept on a cot in the pantry
Every night since his arrival. He has been lost
On the path from the garden to the house eleven times
During this visit alone.

And after an outing to the beach
He bored everyone for three days by claiming
To have invented the rock barnacles, the clear,
Sea cucumbers and the calm, country birds
Mewing above the cliffs. Euphoric and vain,
He praised his own genius in creating over a thousand
Species of hunch-backed sand hoppers and their kin.

This morning he is insisting he was born Frederick
Louis Khalibou Yuit of an Eskimo mother and a caribou father.
He believes that he and Cecil used to run the tundra south
To the taiga with the herd. He says when the moon
Smells of rosettes and herbs, he will sing
All the songs his father taught him,
If he can remember them.

Shocked one afternoon to see Sonia,
Whom he regarded as a character in his novel-in-progress,
Serving cheese and poppy seed pastry at tea,
He had to be restrained forcibly and locked for an hour
In the cupola to calm his attempts to verify her reality.

Some days he grips Cecil's arm for hours at a time.

Cecil has learned how to endure
His second-cousin's visits. Sitting at bedtime
Before the fire, when he asks Cecil if he remembers
How they entered the fire one night together
And danced with sizzling hair, throwing their arms
Like light above their heads, and if he recalls
The night the flying fox came to their nursery window
And whispered to them with the voice of a white spruce,
And if he can still find the scars left when the orange slashes
Of a forest evening struck them both hard across the eyes,
Cecil, with a sigh, always says yes.

Aspects of Unity

I

This morning at tea Cecil said that violet in flowers
Was the color of accumulated moisture.

Gordon has taken his prism to the east window now
And is making small perfect rainbow-lines
All along the white wall opposite. He says violet
Is nothing more than the shortest ray
Of the visible spectrum.

Albert has used the word *violet* five times
In the hour since tea and the word *violent*
Twice in the last ten minutes.

Felicia, standing before the hall mirror,
Believes her eyes are the color of the shortest rays
Of the bellflowers after a heavy summer rain.

Sonia thinks the words *purple* and *violating*
Pronounced together after dark have definite
Sexual implications.

This makes Felicia wonder if the bean
Of the sieva plant is purple in the dark
Before the sun splits its pod.

Cecil knows nipples made purple by the shortest rays
Of the moon shining on a white body on a white sheet
Can never be found or touched during the light of day.

II

The only time Albert, Sonia, Felicia and Cecil
Hold hands together is when they run
Down the aster-covered slope from the house
To the lake after lunch.

Gordon, imagining the violet monkshood
Growing on the tundra today, always carries
His satchel in one hand and never participates in the run.

Sonia is curious as to whether a lavender gull flying over
Will look down at them if they all stare at its dark purple
Wingtips at the same time without blinking.

Felicia says violet eyes make gulls disappear in the evening sky.

Gordon believes the properly trained eye can see the lake
At dusk as synonymous with the tundra
Covered by a continuous bed of lavender monkshood.

Cecil knows a game
In which one purple button among many white ones
Must be identified in the dark by touch alone.

Albert, Sonia, Felicia, Cecil and Gordon
Never think the same thing at the same time,
But sometimes, reading outloud together
In the pale violet light of long winter evenings,
They speak the same words at the same time,
And when they do, all, except Albert,
Call it colorful recitation.

Naked Boys on Naked Ponies

They ride through invisible hollows
And along the indefinite edges of marshy streams,
Fog swirling up to their ears
Over beds of sida and flowering spurge.
The ponies' withers become ivory with pollen
From the blossoming quince, and the bare
Legs of the boys are marked by flickertail
Barley and wild mint. Moisture
On the corn cockle along the ridges
Makes constant suns in their eyes.

Galloping through forests and across fields
Of drying grasses, this is what they create
By themselves—spilled ginseng and screeching
Pipits, dusts rising from the witherod
And the wild raisin, an effusion of broken
Beargrass somersaulting skyward
And mouse-ear chickweed kicked high.

And beside the river they see themselves
On the opposite bank following themselves
Through water chestnuts and willow oak, and they see
Themselves threading among the stand of hornbeam
In the forest ahead. Watching from the precipice
Above the canyon at evening, they know the bronze
Ponies and their riders curving in a line
Along the ledges below.

And at night they see themselves riding upside down
Across the sky, hair and tails and manes
Dragging in the grasses among the long horn beetles

And burrowing owls. And they see themselves galloping
Across the prairie turned upside down, hair
And tails and manes dragging in the dusty glow
Of the starry nebulae. They know they are the definite
Wish of all unexplored spaces to be ponies and boys.

I tell you the speed of the ponies depends absolutely
On the soaring of the rider squeezing tightly
Inside each of their skulls. And the wings of the boys
Depend absolutely on the flight of the ponies
Galloping across the prairies contained in their bones.
And the soaring of the prairies depends absolutely
On the wings of the ponies squeezing tightly
Inside every grass and bone found in the flight of the boys.

And who cares where they are going,
And who cares if they are real or not,
When their ride by itself is that glorious?

The Witness of Death

There was a crisis in the health of Felicia's uncle
During the autumn following his first seizure
Of insanity. Believing himself to be the hoary puccoon
Of the field, how could he endure sitting by the window,
Watching his own slow death advance by dry chill
And musty mold up spine and stem, drawing the throat
Of his blossom tightly closed? What could he suppose,
Seeing the low, cold and quiet sun of the season
Blurring the distinction between stalk and sky,
Obliterating the relationship of petal to earth?

Even wrapped in flannel and fleece and sitting
By the fires, still he shivered stiffly
In the November fogs, whimpering as the damp
Cold evening above the roots eased nearer to his heart.
He complained that his fingertips and ears
Were obviously bitten, shriveled and brown,
The morning after the first heavy frost.

Felicia, wishing to slow his demise,
Closed and locked all the shutters in his room,
But no one could abide the howls
Of his lost soul then left utterly formless,
Bereft of leaf and eye and the steady ritual
Of wasting-away.

Cecil painted a portrait of the hoary puccoon
Of the field in the full orange glory
Of its summer blossom and hung it before his window
As a benevolent ruse. Although the flower
Was glorious and bold in its oils, Cecil failed
To capture on canvas the complete essence of his spirit.
Even Felicia said it wasn't her uncle at all.
The crisis continued.

The day the skin of his face turned as cold
And white as the ice-covered snow over the field
And he lay without trembling for 12 hours straight,
All was considered lost. Then Albert, jumping
From his chair, rushed to the field alone,
Dug through the snow and gathered six whole seeds
From the frozen hoary puccoon. Taking them to Felicia's uncle,
He placed three on his tongue, which he swallowed, and pressed
The others into his tight hoary hand closed beneath the quilt.
(Gordon said his right foot quivered visibly at that moment.)

Now, although Felicia's uncle will not open his eyes,
He sips small amounts of icy water through a thin
Vein-like straw, and he breathes, slowly, unaided
And calm, through every night.

While the doctors and the household prepare for spring,
Sonia comes to kiss the forehead of Felicia's uncle
Everyday, and she touches his temples with perfume
Extracted from the blossom of the hoary puccoon,
Bottled and sent to him, with love, from a well-wisher
Half-way around the world.

The Well-Wisher from Half-Way Around the World

Though everyone knows the well-wisher exists (many
Have trinkets sent by him to prove it), no one has
Seen him or heard his name. Like two figures etched
On the opposite sides of a silver coin,
No one can see himself and the well-wisher
At the same moment.

Nevertheless the naked boys on their ponies
Have set out many times to locate the well-wisher.
But they simply find themselves on the path
Between the sugarwoods and the cliffs
Above the sea or crossing the marble bridge
Over the River of Rhom or sleeping at the eastern edge
Of the summer savannah. The well-wisher always lives
On the opposite side of wherever they are.

Therefore Albert, wading in July among the inlet pools,
Looking for thorny sea stars and rock-boring urchins,
Tries to remember that it is winter, at the moment,
For the well-wisher. And when the shadow
Of the purple finch flying over the lawn is seen
Against the bright grass at noon or when the tunnel
Of light made by Albert's torch suddenly appears
Through the black forest at midnight, Sonia is reminded
That the well-wisher exists.

Sometimes Felicia likes to watch the sunset so long
And so carefully that she can still see its glow
Even after the dimmest star of Andromeda can be found.
She wants to see the last moment of the sun's ending
Exactly as the well-wisher is witnessing
The first instant of its beginning.

Cecil, delirious for a week with a late winter fever,
Believed that he and the day were stretched
From horizon to horizon together in two dimensions,
That there was no chamber pot, no dog asleep
Beneath the bed, there being no other side
To the bed. Unable to pronounce the words *deep*
Or *shallow* or *above* or *below,* his eyes looked
Neither up nor down. It was only after the arrival
Of the star-shaped violets sent by the well-wisher
And the simultaneous breaking of his fever,
That he was able to see inside and outside once more.

The blind beggar, who once spent eleven days
In the Deeper Caverns, claims that during his last hour
Beneath the earth when he finally saw nothing of himself
But his blindness, he almost touched the well-wisher.

Gordon, twirling a coin on the table, believes
That death, like the rapid spinning of a flashing
Silver coin, is the only experience during which the unity
Of opposite surfaces might finally be perceived.

No one can find Kioka in the winter.

Yet Cecil came back from sledding this evening
Believing it was Kioka's body he had seen buried
In brown, reed-like lines under the ice at the pond.

And Felicia, running yesterday morning to the clearing
Where the snowbirds were squabbling,
Said the birds were dusting in the warm ashes
Left from Kioka's fire.

During a February blizzard, Sonia thought
She could hear Kioka's pony stomping and thrashing,
Screaming as if it were tethered in the sleet
In the open field, and she imagined she could hear
Someone on the roof singing the "Song of Lamentation
For Tethered Ponies" that Kioka learned from his father.

Everyone wonders what it means to be Kioka,
Alive in the blizzard, taking the fury of the icy wind
Into his lungs over and over all night, sleeping
Face to face with the sleet. What will he look like
In the spring, having watched the storm thrashing
Like a tethered pony, having screamed himself
Like wind tied to the end of a rope?

Felicia says icicles are simply the vision of the sun
Caught on the blade of Kioka's knife then frozen and multiplied
Across the northern eaves. That's why
She likes to eat them.

All day Tuesday Cecil, hiking in the snow,
Tried to find the hollow tree where he dreamed he saw
The naked body of Kioka curled and frozen,
Covered with the frost of his own breath.

Gordon says a dream is definite proof
Of the physical absence of its subject.

Felicia has written on her chalkboard,
"Winter comes when Kioka is cold."

Albert, who is tired of telling everyone
That Indian imitators definitely don't hibernate,
Found a single red feather this morning lying
On the unmarked snow on the south side
Of the berry hedge.

A Seasonal Tradition

Felicia's music teacher gives a concert for Sonia,
Cecil, Albert, Gordon and Felicia and her insane uncle
In the front parlour every holiday season.
After her traditional repertoire she always plays
One piece on her violin in a register so high
The music can't be heard.

The silence of the parlour during that piece
Is almost complete, broken only by the sputter
Of a candle, a creaking yawn from one of the dogs.

Albert admires the entranced look
On the music teacher's face and the curious trembling
Form of her fingers as she plays. He thinks
He can hear the unheard music in the same way he can hear
Wind among the black strings of the icy willows blowing
In the tundra night. He thinks the silence he hears
Is the same silence found in the eyes of the frogs living
Below the mud at the bottom of the frozen bays.

With tears in her eyes, Felicia says the unheard song
Reminds her of the cries of unborn rice rats
And bog lemmings buried in the winter marsh
And the humming of the white hobble bush blossom still
In its seed and the trill of the unreal bird discovered
In the river trees by the river sun.

Watching the violinist swaying in her velvet gown,
Closing her eyes, pursing her lips, Cecil knows
Sonia is the only possible theme of this composition.

Hoping for a cure for Felicia's uncle, Sonia thinks
The inaudible music might be the unspoken speech
In which he is thought to have lost himself years ago.

At the conclusion of the piece (signaled
By the lowering of the violin) there is always spontaneous
Applause and much barking and leaping by the dogs.

The unheard composition is the one song
Most discussed later over tea and pastries,
And, although it was the subject of the quarrel
During which Cecil knocked Albert's doughnut
From his hand last year, it is still generally considered
The evening's greatest success.

Part II

Being Remembered

For Felicia, they were dancers first, turning
In their tight white trousers and purple sashes
Out of the hardwood forest into the hazy sun.

For Gordon's sake, they complicated the coordination
Of their movements, cartwheeling, somersaulting
In circles, shifting their patterns like colored stones
Tumbling in a glass kaleidoscope.

Cecil wouldn't have noticed them
If they hadn't been wearing red patent leather boots,
Boots that moved across the landscape as they danced
Like quick brushstrokes of scarlet
On a canvas of yellow field.

For the blind beggars they wore seven brass bells
Around their ankles to mark each step,
And for the blind beggars they carried
Tambourines to define the place of their hands
In the afternoon. For the naked boys they pranced
Like ponies to the glacial pool. They drank
Like ponies, shaking their heads with a flourish
At the dark blue edge of the summer ice.

Not one yellow aster in the entire meadow
Would have tightened to its stem if the dancers
Hadn't stopped to spin in the grass, their bright hair
Spreading like the petals of a golden flower.

The star-watchers would never have studied them
If it hadn't been for the black satin shirts
They wore, the five suns flashing
Off the mirrored buttons down the front.

A Modicum of Decorum

Eduard, Felicia's tutor, having read
A current best-seller entitled
The Potential Sophistication of Life and Limb,
Is attempting to improve Felicia's behavior.

He has given her a list.

> Somersaulting and leaping confuse clear-thinking.
> Running and bounding lead to chaos in the brain.
> No one can deny that shrieks destroy
> The most delicately balanced tedium.
>
> Strolling in moderation is tolerated.
> Twisting ribbons and twiddling by small
> Quiet fires is cultivated.
> Sighing is admired.

Eduard, quoting from Chapter IX, has told Felicia
She must envision herself as a heavy, metal bell
Hanging with no pull-cord in a dark, vine-covered
Belfry, her only meaningful reality being the potential
Of her ring. To actually ring then, being the destruction
Of potential and therefore the destruction of meaningful
Reality, is a sin.

Yesterday Felicia, confined to her bedroom
For singing her part in the morning blessing
With too much intensity, wove ropes of pink
And purple crepe-paper and hung them from her window.
There they blew in the breeze beside the veranda
Where Eduard was tentatively meditating on the potential
Reality of ringing in bells not yet forged.
Now he is reading aloud to Felicia Chapter XXIV,
"The Abuses of Flags, Banners, Streamers, Confetti,
And other Paper Paraphernalia."

Felicia, attempting to walk at the pace her tutor
Has approved, thinks if she could camp-out all summer
Heading east, then she might be able to make it
To the field and back once before autumn.

Eduard says a backpack is unseemly.

Last night Felicia, tip-toeing
(which Eduard hasn't yet discussed) across the lawn
To the gazebo, lay inside its latticed walls
With moonlight diamonds covering her body
And giggled with the dogs until dawn.

For Felicia and the
unrealized soul of
her favorite lost
doll.

He should never have been set down all alone
In the field like that, a real clown in his floppy
Satin pajamas, dizzy among the trembling pipewort,
Quavering like the brainless wool grass.
Bone-bald in his black skull cap, perpetual
Astonishment on his white painted face, he sits
And stares, his dark lashes as large as teardrops
Circling each wide eye.

How can he ignore the big clicking buttons
Swinging on his baggy blouse as he bends to pick
A prickly daisy for his lapel, or his long cuffs
Falling into the creek as he studies the bravado
Of a crawdad backing under a leaf? Tripped
On the hill by his own pantaloons, he's already lost
One of his tassel-topped silk slippers in a hedgehog hole.

And the starched ruffle around his neck scratches
His ear as he turns to count the jays screaming
Their nonsense among the awkward oaks. He's been teased
For half an hour by a light-headed butterfly flitting
Just out-of-reach above the raspberry blooms.

Recognizing himself, doesn't he see the wild pantaloons
On the catapulting locust, the bone-tight caps
Of the blackbirds, the white painted faces of the trillium?
He knows the figure he makes sprawled
Among the addle-headed grasses, beside the dumb-struck
Rocks, bewildered under the blank and foolish sky.
He's certain the field is a clumsy buffoon.

Oh, if he could only remember or if he could only
Forget or if he could only imagine someone
Out-of-sight beyond the hill,
Someone who thinks about him always,
Without laughing.

The Study of the Splinter Expert

An expert on splinters was the guest lecturer
Featured at the academy last week. His career began
As a youthful hobby—a curiosity concerning
The minute lines in slivers of oak and ash, an expanding
Collection of glass splinters, purple, scarlet;
Metal shavings.

Spending two years as a student sorting
Through the refuse left from the explosion
Of a single pine, deciphering patterns in that tangled
Fall of feathered wood, he discovered and classified
Fifty varieties of splinters broken from splinters.

His meticulous investigation of the calls
Of the meadowlark splintering the spring afternoon
Led to his first book, *The Splinters of Time.*
Since then he has completed research on the splinters
Of moonlight made by the needles of icy firs, wind
Splintering the silver surface of the lake, the splintering
Of the wind by the blades of the bur-reed.

In any entity he can only see the underlying
Truth of its splintered reality—the red
And yellow splinters composing rattle box
And hibiscus blooms, splinters forming
In the fertile egg of the swamp snake, the potential
Splinters of chill in future snow. He predicts
The eventual development of an instrument able to locate
And describe each splinter of space.

Concerned with the splintering action of analysis itself,
He has carefully studied photographs of himself
Taken as he scrutinized shavings from the femurs
Of unborn calves, shatters of hickory found
Before the rising of the sap. He has attempted
To locate in his own eye that splinter of light
Creating the original concept of "splinter."

Thursday evening he lectured on his recent
Proposal that the sharpest, most painful
Splinter experienced is not of micromagnesium
Or glass silk but the splinter of pure hypothesis.

A well-known seer has predicted that the death
Of this expert will come by steel splinter piercing
His eye and brain, whereby he will enter that coveted state—
The perfect union of object and idea.

Felicia, infatuated with the erudite demeanor
Of the splinter expert, hasn't left her bed during the five days
Since his departure. She is using a calculator to count
The splinters of loss filling the distance multiplying
Between them, and she's afraid that, should she rise,
The splinters of her despair, blending like moonlight
On the floor, would scatter like dust and be lost forever.

The Shape of Sorrow

Felicia wants to contract melancholia today.
She wants to be able to feel her sorrow swelling
Like a shore-line cavern feels the slow rise
Of the sea filling its caves. She wants to say
She is sick with sadness.

Cecil told Felicia that sorrow, when not diffuse,
Is actually the most distinctive physical property
Of hedgerows, marshy shores and thorn fields.
Now she wants to become that single most definite
Point of beauty—the needle of the seed shrimp, the sharp
Motion on each blade of swordgrass—which she believes
Is simply the pure concentration of sorrow.

Gordon has a colleague who is making a study
Of the evolutionary development and social significance
Of tears. Felicia is to be the subject of his next paper.
She is saving her tears in sterile
Vials for chemical analysis.

Today Felicia wants to train her vision
So that she is able to detect the pathos
In the jelly eggs of the swamp chorus frog, in the nuptial
Swarms of dixa midges over the meadow pond. Staring
Plaintively from her bedroom window, she has already learned
To see her sadness as the individual wings
Of each mayfly circling the pepper bushes, to see
Her sorrow as the earth's constant line
Maintaining itself against the sky.

She is beginning to love the words
Dementia praecox.

Sonia thinks it might actually be possible
For someone to compose a lasting blessing
For the virtue and periodicity of sorrow.

Felicia says all of this would be easier
If Albert and the dogs would play
On the other side of the house for a while.

The Clockmaker and the Toymaker are Friends

Because sometimes people want clocks that are toys—
Twelve thimble-sized birds with turquoise feathers
That descend one by one on gold wires to glass
Trees denoting each hour; red, heart-shaped
Clocks sewn inside pillow-bears
Or muslin-breasted princess dolls.

And sometimes people want toys that are clocks—
A three-inch grieving doll in a purple beaded dress
Who wrings her white wax hands second by second;
A motorized drummer who drums at nightfall
And again at dawn; a mechanical gypsy with an ear
For a clock, who turns her head twice each minute to listen.

The clockmaker is fashioning two tiny crystal
Timekeepers for the toymaker to use as eyes
In his next doleful rag clown, thus giving
Vision to time. And the toymaker is making
A spinning ballerina on a pedestal of pearls
So the clockmaker may mark each turn,
Thus giving moment to frivolity.

When the toymaker dreams of clocks, he sees
The silver wheels of gyroscopes, rolling hoops,
Flashing brass trinkets composing the only pure
Mechanism of time. When the clockmaker dreams of toys
He sees counted rows of metal soldiers, lines
Of falling dominoes, a turning jump rope composing
The only true character of play.

Occasionally the clockmaker and the toymaker
Live on opposite sides of the river and do not speak
To one another for months at a time, so that,
Isolated, they may work simultaneously to distinguish
The perfect unity of their separate crafts.

Locating the Source of Intention

Within the crystal bird that Felicia is admiring
In the window of the curio shop this morning
Is a perfect skeleton of glass bones. The moment
Of the bird's intention to fly appears as a bend
Of purple light curved deep within its wing.
And beneath its glass clavicle is a dram
Of salt water wavering and shimmering like a heart.

As Felicia looks closer she can see, inside the bubble
Of the bird's body, a transparent egg holding a perfect curl
Of unborn bird, its bones folded as glistening wing
And femur of glass threads. Beneath the vestige of clavicle
There is a sure but wavering salt-point of light.

Looking further she can see, within the loins
Of that unborn bird, a semblance of egg containing
A skeleton of spider-bird bones, a shimmer
Of purple veins connected like night and a hair-bone
Of light forming as heaven's intention to rise like a wing.

And inside the glistening drop of potential egg floating
Inside that embryo-to-be nestled inside the unborn
Bird folded inside the glass bird inside the shop window,
Felicia can sense a definite breath of bones, a waver
Of night wing and a microscopic explosion of light rising
In her eye as proof of the intention
Of a non-existent heart to see.

Felicia is counting backwards now to discover
How many deaths and how many births will be needed
To fully release that flight.

No one knows where the shop owner finds
Such curios to display behind his window
Or how he locates the glassblower
Who executes them.

The Mystery of Union

Although naked boys and naked ponies
Are definitely two different things, no one has ever
Seen a naked boy off the back of his pony.

Once, in a dense, pre-dawn fog, Gordon thought
He saw a naked boy slipping down over the slick rump
Of his chestnut mare, but as his feet touched
The gold grassy field he disappeared with his horse
As if they had suddenly become glass in the sparkling mist.

And once Sonia was certain she saw a shining pony
Without a boy on its back galloping toward her
Out of the setting sun, but looking closer,
She saw a boy rising from the flames shimmering
Along the pony's spine, rising until he stood upright
On its back, his hair flying like fire as he balanced
With both arms spread wide.

While he was lost in a mountain blizzard,
The oldest blind beggar by the river believes
He saw naked boys, white with frost and blinded
By the ice-filled wind, leading their blindfolded ponies
With ropes along a rocky ledge. But no one
Can ever understand exactly what a blind beggar sees.

Whenever Cecil tries to paint a naked boy
Riding on a naked pony, the first stroke of his brush
Always proceeds from the boy's slender shoulder
Straight down without a break to the pony's hoof.
He cannot execute on canvas a definite line
Dividing the pressure of knees from the trembling
Of withers. He doesn't know a technique
For painting the mane without simultaneously painting
The fingers that grip the coarse, entangling black hair.

It is Gordon's theory that a naked boy dismounted
Does not cease to exist but instead becomes
The invisible message of an earth devoid

Of mounted motion. And the riderless pony
Does not disappear but becomes instead an alternate form
Of its speed which is the static hoofbeat of time
Unnoticed in the heart.

Felicia wants to ride with a naked boy
On his naked pony. She wants to know
If then she will become blind to herself.
Or maybe, while she is riding on the back
Of a naked pony, she will be able to look
Across the prairie and see god watching.

But as for now, it is true that the ponies
Can be seen grazing on the spring horizon faraway.
And the boys are there, leaning down toward the grass,
Stretching full-length along their ponies' glossy necks.
And they watch the locusts spread their wings,
And they take blossoms of red clover and rue
To lace at night through the intertwining dark
Of their long black hair.

Gentlemen of Leisure

Yesterday Felicia put an invitation
In the evening newspaper addressed
To all true Gentlemen of Leisure:

> Please come tomorrow for an afternoon
> Of sedate conversation, coffee,
> Mints and finger croissants.

As the gentlemen arrive, ringing
Once at mid-afternoon, all is prepared.
They place their kid gloves, their chapeaux
And their canes, without clatter, on the marble stand
And proceed to the parlour to seat themselves
On the couch of bruised-rose brocade, the white-lacquered
Chairs and the maroon-cushioned settee.

Felicia thinks the Gentlemen of Leisure
Are magnificently regal in their lavender
Lamb's wool suits and pearl buttons. She adores
Their subtle aromas of unsmoked tobacco, crushed marjoram
And black cinnamon stem.

There are prolonged silences in the parlour
As the gentlemen nod to one another and muse
And abstractly balance their demitasse. They touch
Their temples occasionally with the lace
Of their wine-colored cravats.

They discuss for a moment the brief verse
They discussed during their visit last year.
And they note the shadow of the fern

In its bamboo stand on the dark polished floor.
They recall the rare virgin canary
Which eats small white seeds in the forest
And sips single drops of silver water
In the afternoon and again at dawn.

All true Gentlemen of Leisure are genuinely
And exquisitely calm inside the outer trappings
Of their serenity. Unlike Eduard, who preaches
The code common to all Gentlemen of Leisure,
They know nothing personally of biological petulance
Or preordained harangue.

Cecil wants to paint a portrait
Of the gentlemen sitting and gazing together
In the parlour, but he cannot find the proper shade
Of mauve. And he feels, besides, that the vulgar
Movements of his brush might irreparably violate
The sensitivities of his subjects.

This afternoon, Kioka has insisted
On erecting his sweat-bath tipi on the lawn
Beside the parlour windows. Even though Felicia closes
The drapes, Kioka can still be heard chanting
In the sizzling and sputtering steam that rises
From the glowing rocks. What a triumph
That only one teaspoon rattles against its saucer
As Kioka rushes suddenly from his bath
Screaming his surrender and runs toward the lake!

Doesn't each Gentleman of Leisure sleep well at night,
Cool and scented with rosebay on the smoothest white
Linen, under a coverlet of combed angora, a low light
Burning by his bed in a cut-crystal bowl all night?

Sonia must pray for all true Gentlemen of Leisure
Who lend such glorious affirmation
To passivity.

When they rise to leave, precisely
At the perfect moment of dusk, they hold
Their carved canes lightly and stroll
On the white-pebbled path, slowly through the fog
Just gathering among the budding laurel and the full-flowered
Plum, glancing once this way and once that,
And Felicia holds her breath for the beauty.

Part III

The Effort to Eliminate Ignorance: Birdwatching

Felicia, who can't name the horned lark
Or the Lapland longspur that she has definitely spotted
Across the grasslands, has never been able to see
The chat or the ricebird or the nest of the rock wren
That Albert demands she search for.

Cecil has discovered where sleep exists—
Deep in the center of his own palm. He has seen it
In that creased cavern spiralling
Through stalks of bone. Cecil believes
That the nature of dreams might be revealed
By studying the way the buteo hawk soars skyward
Disappearing into the cupped hand
Of the desert night.

Sonia is compiling a catalog of birds
In which she defines the willet as the first thought
Of wind against the brow, and the godwit
As the manifestation of billowing wheat
Still held in the seed, and the dickcissel as the memory
Of a china tea cup pressed against the lip.
All of her definitions change daily, having monthly
Phases like the moon.

Kioka, who can hear the wheatear when it begins
Its migration southward from the rocky tundra,
Who can smell bayberry on the breath
Of the tree swallow flying overhead and feel the heat
From the domed nest of the king rail across the marsh,
Who can detect, like little flames in his throat,
The rapid respiration of the common snipe,
Says he is not a birdwatcher, has never been a birdwatcher,
And will never consider becoming a birdwatcher.

Gordon contends that birds are simply intermediary figures
In a gradient of winged behaviour proceeding from the purely
Imaginary flight of the electron to the paper-hair

Flutter of the velvet hover-fly to the slope-soaring
Of the falcon to the vacuous white feathers
Of the moon to the dark-edged wing of the pure
Conception of flight itself.

Kioka thinks if the correct definition of bird is
"A warm-blooded vertebrate with feathers and wings,"
Then when he dances against the canyon sky wearing
His cape made from feathers of the black-necked stilt
And the black-legged kittiwake, then he at least
Ought to be mentioned in Sonia's catalog.

Seminar

"Dominoes, Zebras and The Full Moon"
Are the subjects of the month-long seminar
Gordon is attending at his alma mater.

His first letter home contained the following information:

> Upon entering the speaking hall, each participant
> In the seminar must carry a small banner indicating
> His primary field of expertise—
> Black with white stripes for general zebra experts;
> Black with white dots for domino aficionados;
> Pure white for professors of the full moon;
> White with black stripes for authorities investigating
> The effects of zebras on the full moon and vice versa;
> White with white-striped black dots for professors
> Studying the effects of dominoes on zebra experts;
> Descending circles of alternating black and white
> For champion muggins players experiencing
> Recurring dreams of zebras;
> White-striped black with black white-dotted
> Dots for all authorities on seminar banners.

> A single banner is allowed each participant.
> No two participants with the same banner
> May speak in sequence.

On the first day a domino expert rose to speak, saying,
"Some black bones of dominoes possess many full moons,
But the deepest side of any domino never
Has a moon of any kind."

This was immediately challenged by a zebra expert claiming,
"There may be more than one undiscovered moon
On the deepest side of any particular zebra bone."

At this moment, an attendant, wheeling a zebra skeleton
Into the auditorium, broke it into pieces
When he tripped on the ramp and fell.
This unfortunate accident, however, led

To Gordon's conclusion that assembling the pieces
Of a zebra skeleton on a stage is remarkably similar
To laying-out matched domino bones on a table.
Upon presenting this insight with all of its implications
To his colleagues, Gordon received a standing ovation.

And when the last bone of the skeleton
Was finally put into place, someone in the audience
Actually shouted out, "Domino!"

Everyone is eagerly awaiting Gordon's second letter
Which will contain news of the preparations being made
For the all-night rodeo and domino tournament
To be held under the full moon.

Because of her intense interest in this seminar
And her great admiration for Gordon, Felicia
Has despised Albert for most of this month.

The Pursuit as Solution

Whenever Albert is bored, he says he wants to know
What's on the other side of the mind. He says
He sometimes has a vision of himself entering
A bird's throat without injuring it, descending
Deeper and deeper headfirst into that warm black center
Until the pressure building at his feet begins to pull
The whole meadow in behind him, every hop clover
And featherfoil and smartweed and swamp candle.
And then the hills follow with their grey-green rocks,
Their shag barks, bitternuts, sourwoods and birches.
And the iron fence around the lawn and the latticed
Arbor house are sucked in too and the warm perfume
Of guests for dinner, crystal salt shakers,
Embroidered napkins. The whole evening sky
Is taken as if it were a net filled with lapping honeybees,
Bot flies, horntails, shrikes and scaups. And even his dreams
Of flying wingless into space and the invisible and the unlikely
And finally light itself are funneled in. Then the bird,
In that vacuum remaining, begins to enter its own throat,
Followed by Albert himself diving in behind himself
And Albert's mind turned inside out.

Sonia thinks Albert should pick
One small thing such as a ceramic thimble
Or a brass button from his great-great-granduncle's
Naval uniform or a six-spotted fishing spider
And try to find the other side of that first,
For practice.

Albert is happy with this suggestion, and now,
On this Tuesday afternoon, he isn't bored any longer
But is out searching along the seashore for a perfect
Short-spined sea urchin or a spiral-tufted
Bryozoan or a trumpet worm or a sea mouse
With which to begin.

Gordon says this whole idea is ridiculous.
Once Albert *knows* what's on the other side of his mind,
It won't be on the other side any longer.

Entomological Research

Cecil thinks the desert blister beetle
Is simply a single moment frozen in the hard-shelled
Body of a bug, a moment grateful to be given
A blue metallic head and six purple legs.
He thinks by watching an entire nest of disturbed beetles
One might see history rearranging itself.

Sonia thinks each purple blister beetle
Is the six-legged proof of a running entomological discussion
Between the desert floor and the sun.

Albert knows the desert blister beetle he studies
Is nothing but the brain finally seeing itself
As the possibility of insect it has always been.

The underside of any brain then
Must be the blue luminescent belly
Of the blister beetle flipped over on its back.

Occasionally Felicia wonders what Albert's brain is
As it recognizes itself in the act of becoming
The hunched-backed blister beetle it studies.

If the blister beetle could perceive itself
As the subject of this research, then its brain might become
The perfect physical image of the words,
Six purple legs and a blue metallic head.

The brain, surrounded by the sun, the desert floor
And the blister beetle it becomes, definitely knows
How to make itself the subject of any entomological discussion.

Someone, grateful for a change in this discussion,
Could suggest that if each blister beetle represented
A note of duration on the musical scale,
Then a startling symphony of revelation
Might exist unheard on the desert floor.

Gordon, with his ear to the sand,
Has told everyone to be quiet twice.

The Love of Enchantment: Felicia Was Kissed in the Garden Last Night

Someone unseen behind her in the sage
And iris odors of the gravel pathway
Definitely took her by the shoulders,
Pushed her hair aside carefully and kissed her
With decision and concern just once,
There at the darkness below her ear.

And there was breath in that kiss
As if the hesitation and impetuosity
Of spring together had finally found
One motion. And there was love
In that motion like the parting
And reconciliation inside a hawthorne seed
Finally divining together a branch
Full of blossoms.

And now, by her belief in the imagined spell
Created by that kiss, Felicia clearly perceives
The means by which the earth can be taut
With Indian pipe, heavy with the matted roots
Of salt marshes, dark with redwood shadows,
While at the same moment it can soar, clean
And shining, a white grain sailing
In the black heavens around the sun.

A new resiliency has risen in Felicia's bones
Since her encounter in the garden, a warm
And dominant, marrow-related alloy sustained
By her spine remembering those fingertips brushing
Her shoulders with praise. Everyone recognizes
The new buoyancy of esteem in the charmed energy

And sureness of her body swimming across
The lily-bordered lake this evening.

Now even Gordon wants to see and touch
That small exalted, transfigured,
Lip-defined, miraculous moment of her neck.

And no one is sorry that, even if just once,
Felicia was kissed and cherished that way
In an ordinary garden rightly declared, rightly
Proclaimed, justifiably announced by Felicia, running
To clasp both of Albert's hands in her own,
As grandly enchanted last night.

How the Whale Forgets the Love of Felicia

If he breaches at all, he only rises
To a moderate height, rolls little
And falls without luster or surf, silently
In an unremarkable mid-autumn fog.

He rejects the underlying form
Of the fairy shrimp, will not ingest
Fleeing krill if their silver bodies sparkle,
Ignores the possibilities in the strong,
White wings of the manta ray.

In order to avoid the awareness
Of her absence, he must not close his eyes.
In order to avoid the sound of her name,
He must not remind himself to forget.

He deliberately pulls away and by-passes
Brilliant bars of green sun shimmering
Through the dark sea, and he pulls away and sinks
Deliberately from the light salt-vacancies
Of stars ascending like tiny jewels of air
Through the ocean night.

And he never pictures the beauty of barefoot
Riders on horseback when white gulls perch
And flutter on his crusty hump.
And he never remembers tireless dancers
In transparent silks when white waves leap,
Reaching and bowing before a violet sky.

As he moves forward, he doesn't heed or acknowledge
The only direction manifested naturally and forever
Inside the tough hide of his heart, and he doesn't name

The honor of his own broad brow or the honor
Of the comb jellies he passes or the bravery of the bream
And the halfbeaks or the cruelty of the moon's soft skin
Sliding along his own in the night.

How careful he must be never to profess with fervor
The devotion of denial, the clear affirmation
Of suffering.

Indifferent to his own methods, he merely dives
Repeatedly to a depth of dull twilight
Where he meditates without passion on the great
Indeterminable presence of the steady sea, the rock
And return, the capture and simultaneous release
Of its thousand, thousand meaningless caresses.

In the month of March, Albert plans
An expedition up the eastern side
Of the nearest mountain.

Kioka says bands of Peruvians coming down
The mountain have reported seeing flocks of hummingbirds
In a meadow near the summit, hummingbirds
With invisible wings, blue-green heads and thumb-bellies
Of scarlet-orange. Kioka believes the trumpet vines
That cover the meadow have swallowed the wings
Of the hummingbirds.

Albert thinks that the hummingbirds, if they exist,
Have changed themselves into Peruvians with ponchos
Of blue-green and scarlet-orange thrown over their shoulders,
That they have come down from the mountain
To repeat their own legends.

The Peruvians seem to go easily up and down
The mountain as if they had invisible wings.
And they themselves say that their women
Go up to the meadow alone to mate
With the hummingbirds in May. They claim their babies
Nurse on trumpet blossoms in the meadow
Until they are old enough to fly.

According to legend,
The ancient Peruvian word for nipple is
Sweet-nectared blossom of orange.

Last fall a black-eyed woman by a mountain road
Gave Sonia a basket of trumpet blossom vines
And old hummingbird nests. Scarlet-gold yarn

And bits of turquoise wool could be seen woven
With spider silk among the threads of the old nests.

Sonia likes to think that hummingbirds are simply
Scarlet-orange trumpet blossoms clipped from the vine,
Given invisible wings and green tongues, that their bellies
Are always full of their own honey.

The title of Cecil's most recent oil painting is
Green Hummingbird Tongue Licking an Orange Nipple.

Gordon is looking through his magazines
For an article entitled "An Analysis of Nectar,
With a View toward Predicting the Structure
Of the Creatures it Sustains."

Sometimes Felicia waits beside the lake at dawn
Until the sky is the exact color of trumpet blossoms.
Then she imagines she is the wing of a hummingbird
Caught inside the orange stomach of a flower
Or a Peruvian baby wrapped in a wool nest, nursing
At her mother's breast.

"Hummingbirds Speaking with Peruvian Tongues"
Is the title of an old song without words.

Albert is spending every day now assembling
And checking his gear. He has ordered bird traps
And vine clippers. And every night Gordon falls asleep
Working on his newest book, *Scarlet-feathered
Flowers and Egg-producing Vines in the Legends
Of the Upper Andean Plains.*

Felicia has had a telescope mounted at her window
And will watch for Albert's campfire every evening
In March. He will set a lone pine ablaze at the summit
If he has seen hummingbirds or Peruvians,
And he will shoot an orange flare into the sky
If either has spoken.

Kioka will accompany him, traveling
Out of sight without fire.

It's only January.
"Legend Full of Its Own Nectar" is the name
Of this winter.

The Facts of the Earth

(Taken from an entry
found in a partially
burned journal buried
among the ruins of an
old country house)

Every black-lined shadow of each brown grama grass,
Every winged flicker of every beetle wasp
And sawfly, every stickery slice and quilled seed
Of the multitudinous field is a stark
And isolated detail existing entirely by itself,
And there is no field.

And the field is one solid indistinguishable blade
And blend of brown, a stationary broad wash of constant
Blurred wind, a wide, dull entity of motion
With not a single detail of its own,
And there is no field.

And all parts of the giant crack willow—the lance-like
Leaves and the hairy yellow catkins—are noisy and glaring
And irritable with sunlight, and all parts of the giant
Crack willow—the lance-like leaves and hairy yellow catkins—
Are mute and invisible and irritable with shadow.

The grassland sparrows have abandoned their rufous
Caps and their scarlet bills and are not birds at all,
And the grassland sparrows have irrevocably joined themselves
With their scarlet bills and their rufous caps
And are not birds at all.

Felicia, stationary with her arms at her sides, says
It must be the earth spinning slower and slower around her
That causes such weight.

Albert has disappeared.

Cecil says he has no name.

And for a moment, Sonia thinks that salt
Moving by itself from her eyes, over her cheeks,
Is the most inexplicable phenomenon in the universe.

Gordon is dead.

Part IV

The Myth: Raison d'Être

Some say there are wild white ponies
Being washed clean in a clear pool
Beneath a narrow falls in the middle
Of the deciduous forest existing
At the center of the sun.

Some say the thrashing of those ponies
Straining against their bridles, the water flying
From their stamping hooves in fiery pieces
And streaks rising higher than the sandbar willows
Along the bank, drops whirling like sparks
From the manes of their shaking heads,
And the shouting and splashing of the boys,
Yanked off their feet by the ponies
As they attempt to wash the great shoulders
And rumps of those rearing beasts, as they lather
Their necks and breasts, stroking them,
Soothing them, all are the sources of the fierce
Binding and releasing energy existing
At the core of the sun.

The purple jays, mad with the chaos,
Shrieking in the tops of the planetrees,
The rough-winged swallows swerving back
And forth in distress, the struggle of the boys
To soap the inner haunch, to reach
Beneath the belly, to dodge the sharp
Pawing hooves, the wide-eyed screaming
Of the slipping ponies being maneuvered
For the final rinse under the splattering falls,
All the fury of this frightening drama,

Some believe, is contained and borne steadily
Across the blue sky strictly by the startling
Light and combustion of its own commotion.

But when those ponies stand, finally quiet,
Their pure white manes and tails braided
With lilac and rock rose, the boys asleep
On their backs, when they stand,
Fragrant and shimmering, their forelocks
Damp with sweet oil, serene and silent
In the motionless dark of the deep
Riverside forest, then can't everyone
Easily see and understand the magnificent
Silhouette, the restrained power, the adorned,
Unblemished and abiding beauty
That is the night?

The Accounting

Under the wheel of the gypsy's winter wagon
Or covered with desert sand beside Kioka's footprints,
Felicia is said to have found again the journal
That was lost twice. Although she never recognizes
The old-fashioned hand or the strange spelling
That has dated each entry, she believes in the names
She guesses are written there. And she likes
The journal's binding, the odor rising from its pages
Like soil just given light, like wind coming
From the freshly-opened center of an old, old star.

Albert doubts the existence of the journal,
As no one has ever seen it but Felicia,
And she has difficulty reading it, claiming
That every page is too narrow and too fine
For her eyes.

On a blue velvet bookmark given to Felicia
By the gypsies is this saying sewn in sequins:
"Words are remarkably similar to stars
In their ability to determine the past and contain
The future."

Kioka has been lost twice himself
On the desert, walking all night over wide
Sand under a turning wheel of winter stars.
In his own recognizable hand, he has written
On a rock never found again: "One foot
Is named time and one foot is named motion."

If the journal is found again far in the future
And opened to a date far in the past,
Where will Sonia and Cecil be then? found

In the freshly cut center of an old, old star? or lost
In the opened clasp of an unrecognized hand?
Or taken into light like a leaf of soil?

At the desert's far rim Cecil can recognize time as a word
Turning like a wheel so narrow and fine
That edgewise it can't be seen.

Felicia hasn't seen the journal now since she left it
Last night covered with starlight, closed
And locked as tightly as a fine wheel and its word
Turning at the center of an imaginary rock.

She has told Gordon, looking straight into his old
Star-spun eyes, that until she can read in the journal
An account of herself finding a journal twice lost
In which she then discovers an account of herself
Staring into fine, beloved stars, reading her name
Placed on the page like a binding mark between motion
And time, she won't imagine a word of it.

The Evolution of Freedom

Hands, having freed themselves from water and webs,
From the need to support the body, being finally capable
Of placing, by their own fingers, a ring on every finger,
Wish now for a release from blood and bones,
From the odious limitations of arms.

Every summer evening Gordon searches among the trees
For a completely pure cicada, just one red-eyed locust
That is nothing at all but "insect."

As Sonia watched the ostrich of the Kalahari Desert dance
In the first returning rains, she believed
She had never seen water before.

The eye of the insect watching summer
As it places the evening in ring upon ring among the trees
Is already supporting much more than itself.
Gordon understands pure water to be nothing at all
But the desert released from its own limitations.
The ostrich searches the freedom of the rain with its wings
As if it had never seen hands before.

The Revelation of the Willed Hallucination

Cecil plans to watch the next garden party
From the roof of the highest turret overlooking
The courtyard. He wants to see how the silk parasols
Of all the ladies will look when viewed from above—
The perfect, coral, silk-fringed circle of one, the scarlet,
Crystal-beaded sphere of another, the lavender-jeweled,
The turquoise-tinged ivory, the barely turning, pale,
Yellow chiffon. He thinks the parasols, spined like leaves,
Spiked in the center with pistils, bobbing
And swaying slowly among each other on their invisible
Stems will look, from above, like ruffled blossoms
With silk-skirted feet.

Eventually Cecil wants to imagine that he is looking down
On a garden of moving flowers, as if he were seeing
A full field in spring blossom. He might decide then
To name each parasol as he watches. The splay of orange
Brocade he might call the red-orange wood lily
With its black spots. He thinks he will be able to find
The golden, thread-leaved sundew and identify the wild coffee,
The blackberry lily, the hedge mustard and the rosebay.
He will locate the flower of the bindweed spreading
Its yellow stripes exactly from the center of its pink
Satin dome. The pale, yellow chiffon he might call
The sister of the wild senna.

Cecil wants to concentrate on the parasols
Until he can't be certain they are parasols at all,
Until he can't be sure that their silk isn't really
The soft skin of spread petals, until he begins to believe
That the flowers possess hidden breasts beneath their parasols,
That the fine ladies contain in the deepest crevices
Below their petals, spores and pollen and possibilities
Of faint perfumes, until he is convinced it would be possible
To gather a bouquet of small parasols and place them in a vase
On the piano where they might converse as corydalis,
White laurel, the deep-lined purple and blue-eyed grass.

Finally, in the middle of the party, Cecil plans to startle
Everyone by sounding his brass gong from the rooftop.
He believes at this moment the flowers, non-committal
And indifferent so far in the garden below him,
Will suddenly allow the silk circles of their petals
To fall simultaneously in a unique event revealing
For the first time their eyes and mouths and cheekbones,
The complete, bright astonishment of their upturned faces.

The Creation of Sin

Gordon wants to commit a sin
Never committed before. He says he is bored
By the lascivious; he has slept through
A thousand adulteries. He calls theft
And murder and greed embarrassingly unimaginative.

He spends an hour each clear afternoon
On the lawn beneath the alders, grooming the dogs,
Trying to imagine a sin so novel
It has not yet been forbidden.

Sometimes, in the moment just before he discerns
The fish treading in light at the bottom
Of the spring or when he studies the eye
Of the short-eared owl in the instant before it sees
The shrew, he is certain he has already committed
That peculiar sin without knowing it. In the early morning,
As he watches himself from the icy black cedars
By the window, dreaming in his sleep, he can almost
Define it.

As the sole author of a sin,
Gordon knows he would be obligated to create
Its expiation by himself. Grace by seaside scrutiny
He might claim, forgiveness by clam classification,
Confession by continual shell collection.
He could invent sacred vows—sworn custodian
Of conifers, promised caretaker of ambush bugs
And toad bugs. He could preach atonement by paper
And mathematics, redemption by ritual
Guessing at the matter of stars.

Today he has recorded a unique grassland prayer
On a tape with the whooping cranes. He has gathered
Sacraments of metamorphic meal moths and hardening
Sassafras fruit. And he knows if he could just commit
A truly original sin, it would mean the beginning
Of his only real salvation.

One in Three

Although Sonia believes her friend, Lettina,
Is a girl visiting from a coastal city, Kioka
Knows a tree that was once a figurehead
Named Lettina. It stands now in the forest on a rising
Hillside like a wooden girl standing upright on the bow
Of a ship, her skirts blowing around her legs
In soft-leafed branches like the pale green
Billowing remembered by a tree sailing
Like a girl through a forest spring.

Consequently, Kioka believes he is the only one
Who knows how to see the depth of the ocean
In the dark seed-point of Lettina's eyes. And he can hear
The salt swelling in the full leaf forming the circumference
Of her heart. He can find the grain of the tree
In Lettina's palm, the flesh frozen as the lapping
Of the sea stopped in wood.

And in the forest, he can put his hand on the trunk
Of the tree and feel how it shudders
In exactly the same way the sea trembles
Beneath a quivering figurehead, in the same way
Lettina grips the bedpost in the middle of the night
Whenever heavy clouds, like great whales, pass by,
Sounding in the dark. It is one and the same
Sinking that exists in the figurehead plunging
Between cold stormy waves and in the tree
Falling between icy crests of winter light
And in Lettina descending into the cold
Drowning of her dreams.

In the core of the tree Kioka has found
The two wooden crosses the figurehead holds
Toward the sky as she races over the seas
Into the center of the still forest, into the crux

Of Lettina's name. Only Kioka sees how a wooden
Figurehead and a single tree in the forest and Lettina
Can rise together as one, facing straight-on the direction
From which their only motion proceeds.

Before her visit comes to an end, Cecil
Wants to paint a portrait of Lettina, depicting
A detailed chronology of the metamorphosis
Of the tree from seed to flower or vice versa,
Illustrating simultaneously the history
Of female figureheads on clipper ships and the evolving
Essence of Lettina's soul, but no one (Kioka never truly
Understands the meaning of the question) will tell him
Where to begin.

Albert, Standing in the Forest at Night,
  Asks Himself, "Where Did I Come From?"

And the salt-matches in the dark
Of his blood answer silently like the fireflies
Mating in the yaupon hedge before him.

And the shimmerings of a thousand pale moons,
Like poplar leaves blowing in the copse
Across the clearing, answer, "From the stem-and-leaf
Architecture of his flickering
Heart-notion of moment."

And the invisible Angel of Eternity
In his groin repeats, "Out of everlasting light
Broken into time by seeds of white violet
Scattered on the forest floor."

And the fish flashing like soft slips of mica
In the stream, schooled like a synthesis
Of darting, form suddenly as one, a new sentence
Of explanation, adroit and gold-scaled
And lively in Albert's brain.

The image of an Indian standing among the willows
Silently declares, "Out of Kioka's hands
Forming 'Albert' in the ancient sign-language
Of his people."

And the distance from the nearest side of his being
Across the void to the farthest side of his being says,
"Originating from the length the whippoorwill's call
Must travel between the nearest white oak
And the farthest white oak where its echo
Waits in the dark."

And with Albert's own accent, his ear,
Designed by forest winds and night crickets,
Is saying to him, "All is born, all born, immediately
And instantaneously with that question."

Felicia is not really a girl
But a slender stalk of stationary coral,
Particularized yet singular, statuesque
In her tolerance of crabs nesting in her cavernous
Hair, of fish hovering in the shelter
Of her golden flesh. She is dependably columnar
Among the petals of light falling
Around her through the green sea.

Albert is not a real boy but the net
Of a casting spider flying in a wide silver arc,
Weightless, billowing like dawn
In the morning sky.

Sonia is not a girl but the color of wine
Wherever and whenever she is detected—deep
In the tight fingertips of the pink-frilled
Morning glory or beneath the tremulous beak
Of the becard or, on icy February evenings, edged
In black trees along the tops of the frozen hills.

Not an authentic Indian, Kioka is the perfect
Image of himself in buckskin and braids. He even believes
The seven tales he tells of how he touched the abyss
Seven times with his coup-stick hewn
From a seven-year hickory.

Cecil is a salt-grey ocean bird hanging
Like an isolated wave in the sky. His rookery
Is built in cliffs so high the light of the sea
Takes three days to reach it. He knows it is the sight
Of his own tears that tells him when to mourn.
It is by the sound of his own song that he learns
When to celebrate.

These are the roles and this is the cast
Chosen to perform them in a drama entitled
A Brief Glimpse of Reality, written by Gordon,
Posing as an author, in rehearsal now
For its opening night at 8:30 pm on New Hallows Eve.

Kioka rides his brown spotted pinto with naked boys
On naked ponies. They were his darlings
From the beginning, his darlings. Their stomachs
Pressed to the ponies' warm backs, their bare
Heels kicking, every one of them rides fast
With both hands free. Nothing will stop them.
They have the whole wide flat prairie of flowering bluet
Before the house, and they have the whole wide shining
Shore of sand before the sea.

Sonia, Gordon and Albert hurry to the second-story
Veranda to watch the naked boys on their ponies
Whenever they gallop past.

Gordon is pleased to discover that the dark
Blind column of the porch where he places his hand
For a moment contains all the knowledge anyone could pursue
Concerning the galloping hooves of ponies bounding
Over a blue prairie with naked boys on their backs.

Even though Felicia is asleep on a distant hillside
And cannot see or hear the ponies, still it is Kioka
Riding with naked boys who makes the only wide prairie
Of Felicia's heart. It is Kioka who gallops without stopping
Along the only wide shining shore of her heart.

Sonia wants to bring the blind beggars
To the second-story veranda when the ponies pass
So that they may watch the wind coming
Through those flower-filled manes to blow
Against their faces, so that they can see, thereby,

The course of their only cure. And she wants the deaf
Beggars to come and grip the prairie-filled porch railing
During that passing so that they may hear
The only method of their healing.

As the ponies pass, Albert, having removed
All his clothes, stands with his eyes closed
And his ears stopped and grips the column
Of the porch as he rises simultaneously and leaves
The second-story veranda to gallop past himself
On a wild pinto pony following Kioka toward the sea.

Cecil has climbed to the highest garret of the house
So that he can see how Kioka and his ponies reach the bay,
How nothing on the sky or the shore hesitates
As they continue straight out over the water, galloping
Across the waves, through the light-filled spray,
Their hooves striking hard against the flat sun on the surface
Of the sea, how they ride high above the deep, becoming
A rearing, surging line of ocean rim racing along the sky.
He leans forward watching them into the evening, watching
Until they pass so far out-of-sight that he can hear them clearly,
Screaming and thundering and roaring at his back.